SHADOWS

Doyle H. Wyatt

ISBN 978-1-63814-014-6 (Paperback)
ISBN 978-1-63814-015-3 (Digital)

Covenant Books, Inc.
11661 Hwy 707
Murrells Inlet, SC 29576
www.covenantbooks.com

Dedication

This short volume is dedicated to other Vietnam veterans who may recognize some of the situations and feelings described. It is also dedicated to the veterans of all the brushfire wars we have been engaged in from the first Persian Gulf War to the present.

Veterans of WWII were treated with the respect and courtesy their service and sacrifice deserved. That simply has not been true for those who have served their country since that time. The sad truth is that few Americans know much about the men and women engaged in the conflicts that have occurred in the past 30 years or so, and even fewer care.

It would be wonderful if America could remain aloof from the actions of tyrants and power-hungry dictators, but as the most powerful nation on earth that simply is not possible.

The men and women who fight in these shadowy conflicts are not responsible for them but are simply serving as they have been asked to do. For that they deserve the respect of their fellow citizens.

SHADOWS

We went to war—those years ago:
    Andy Hardy sentiment
    John Wayne courage
    Philip Sousa marches;
Adventure was its name!

Then came the heat, the fear, fatigue and death:
    Hardy was a fool
    Wayne a lie
    Sousa a strutting peacock;
Loss was all we gained.

DHW

INTRODUCTION

In early September 1970, my plane landed in California. My beautiful wife was waiting, the day was perfect, and I no longer had to wonder if the next day would see me alive or dead. My year in Vietnam was over. At least that is what I thought.

My service in that war offers nothing to distinguish it. I have no Purple Heart for physical wounds, no major medal for heroism. In fact, I have only the standard ribbons for service there plus the Marine Corps Combat Action Ribbon and one minor award for action in combat. In short, I am like most Americans who served all or part of their Vietnam tours in combat and did their jobs faithfully, but never encountered those extraordinary circumstances that make "heroes" of very ordinary men and women.

What I also have in common, I believe, with many Vietnam vets is the sense of use and betrayal. The feeling of having been duped by our own strong patriotic convictions only to be rejected by the very country we served for the very service we rendered.

This writing will, I hope, make these feelings clearer to those who did not serve in that divisive conflict and help other veterans deal with their own feelings of use and rejection.

Most of my rancor is gone. However, the feeling of betrayal was so complete, and so recently reinforced, that it may be impossible for all of it to ever be gone.

Unless some readers hurry to the wrong conclusion, let me quickly add that I have never climbed a tower and shot people, or hid away in some jungle, or buried myself in a narcotic stupor. Of course, in spite of media reports to the contrary, very few of us ever did such things. This falls into that area of myth like so many others concerning Vietnam and Vietnam veterans. These myths continue the disservice of obscuring the fact that most of us lead productive lives even though we carry the burden of having participated in America's only "lost" war.

Lawson, Missouri, to which my parents moved in 1952 when I was 7 years old, was a lovely farming town of some 500 friendly people and one town drunk. It had three family owned and operated grocery stores, one bank, two feed stores, one lumber yard, a dime store, and a few other business concerns. It was the kind of place where everyone walked to the post office for their mail and everyone knew everyone else which, strangely to some people, offers a kind of freedom difficult to describe. My mother rarely worried about where I was or what I was doing because no matter where I was, it was probably safe unless I was working over-time to make it otherwise. Few people locked their doors and many left their keys in their cars at night. There was no police force, only one unarmed and non-uniformed night watchman, but not much went on and there was little need for concern.

Most of my days were spent on my bicycle, either working as a delivery boy at a local grocery store, or just for the fun of it, or walking the woods and fields with my rifle. This was the life and what could be better than defending my country just like John Wayne. After all, good and bad were clearly defined in my mind and, at that time, in the collective conscience of the country.

Growing up in those surroundings, entertained by movies like *Sergeant York, Sands of Iwo Jima, Flying Leathernecks,* and immersing myself in books such as *God is My Co-Pilot,* it is little wonder that I developed a strong belief that America was the best country on earth, and serving in the military was one of the highest callings possible.

When I was in the 6th grade our teacher took us to the Lexington, Missouri, airport, which was managed by her father. With some coaxing by the other mothers, and considerable begging on my part I was permitted to take my first plane ride. Although I loved the view of the neat, straight rowed farm fields along the Missouri River, the thought of being in the air was a little frightening. But by age 15, when a friend took me for a ride in his Aeronca Champ, the view and the 3-dimensional freedom captivated Me and I could think of nothing but serving my country as a fighter pilot! Since I had come to consider fighter pilots as an elite group, and the Marine Corps as the same, being a Marine fighter pilot would make me the elite of the elite. My course was set, I had to be a jet fighter pilot in the United States Marine Corps.

At age 16 I soloed and got my Student Pilot's License. Little interested me other than flying. High school and college were nothing more than hurdles to be overcome on my way to the cockpit of my very own fighter plane. Of course, I would be the best pilot ever to maneuver a fighter on to the tail of an enemy and, undoubtedly, I would become an ace many times over.

The first step to the cockpit was to become an officer. After acceptance by the Corps for officer training, I spent the summers between three college years at Quantico, Virginia, in the roughest training I could ever have imagined. There were times when I really thought the NCO's and officers who ran the program were trying to kill us. Several of my platoon washed out. In fact, the Sergeants were constantly reminding us that we were college men and didn't have to put up with this terrible treatment. All we had to do was tell them we wanted to DOR (Drop on Request), and we would be on our way home that very day. Some took them up on the offer and others failed for physical reasons, but some of us decided we would not let these homicidal maniacs cheat us out of our dream even if it had become something of a nightmare.

When I received my Bachelor of Arts degree, I also was given my commission as a Second Lieutenant of Marines. After a short leave, I reported to Pensacola Naval Air Station to begin the long process that would lead me to a view of the world from 40,000 feet at Mach two. There was one small catch I had noticed in the literature, but to which I had paid little attention. The Marine Corps and Navy together make up the United States Naval Service (this is not exactly the way the Navy might explain it), and so Marine pilots are trained at Navy facilities. The Navy, by definition, operates in proximity to various large bodies of water. Swimming then becomes of paramount importance and I couldn't swim. To say that the swimming expertise demanded by the Navy in its flight training program is rigorous is putting it mildly. Basic swimming includes 200 meters of the four basic strokes (50 meters each), the Dilbert Dunker (a devise in which a cockpit section slides down a ramp and then flips upside down in the water giving the flight candidate a few seconds to unfasten his harness and get out), a mile swim in a flight suit, a minor thing called the helicopter pick-up, and 30 minutes of treading water and drown-proofing. Once these simple objectives are met, the candidate is taken to the Gulf of Mexico for survival swimming. Suffice it to say that I did not make it to the gulf. Although I volunteered to sacrifice myself should I ever ditch at sea, the Lieutenant Colonel who made such decisions refused my offer and I washed out of flight training. I have never forgotten the feeling of being 23 years old and watching a dream of 8 years duration shatter like fine crystal. It was my first major disappointment in life and was to have far reaching consequences. Now I was a 2Lt of Marines who would never fly a fighter plane and it was back to Quantico for 6 months of training as an infantry officer. Although I felt supremely confident to function as a fighter pilot, I felt no such confidence to lead an infantry platoon. After graduation from BASIC School I volunteered for artillery training and departed for Fort Sill, Oklahoma, for 13 weeks of training in the big guns. This was not an MOS (Military Occupational Specialty), for which I had any real enthusiasm, but then I didn't have much interest in anything at that point.

At the beginning of September in 1969, after saying goodbye to my wife of 3 months, I departed for Vietnam and my assignment as an artillery FO (forward observer), with an infantry company. Since I knew of three other Lieutenants who had died doing the same job, I did not expect to survive and gave my father specific instructions concerning my burial. This was done during a long walk so as not to cause my mother undue anxiety. Strangely, I did not consider the anguish it might cause my father.

Like most veterans, the first things to assail my senses on arrival were the heat, humidity, and odor. If I forget everything about Vietnam, the smell of decay, death, and the burning residue of GI outhouses is forever etched in my brain. Once in the bush I found that the aroma of human and animal waste was as much a part of the country as the rice and the beautiful, dark-eyed children.

All the movies of World War II showed officers of supreme confidence leading their men in successful attacks employing tactics which showed a total understanding of their men, their weapons, and the terrain (at the time I forgot this was partly due to a well written script and a good director). As I stood in the stifling heat of Danang, I just prayed no Marine would die because of any ineptitude on my part. It's one thing to be the proud Marine Lieutenant on leave or walking through the airport terminal, but quite another when those gold bars had better translate into leadership in the most demanding environment imaginable.

Shortly after debarking from the airliner I reported to the headquarters of the 5th Marine Regiment for assignment. As an artillery officer I would be assigned to either a direct or indirect support battery. Since I had heard that Lieutenants serving with 105mm and 155mm batteries had a better chance of being selected for in-country training as an AO (Air Observer), I opted for that route hoping to find myself, eventually, in light observation helicopters or the OV-10 fixed wing aircraft. The next day I was on a CH-53 heavy helicopter flying to a village/base ringed with concertina wire, called An Hoa. It was home to several artillery batteries, various other units, and an airfield used by both military planes and Air America (read CIA). Although I was supposed to be given three days to get acclimated and equipped, the next day found me on my way to join a rifle company in the field following the wounding of their FO during the night. I trudged off to war looking more like a little boy running away from home, than like a tough, determined Marine officer. Since there had been no time to equip me, I was wearing stateside utilities and boots, carrying my meager supplies in a snoopy blanket over my shoulder, and was armed with a .45 auto pistol which rattled so that I was afraid firing it would prove fatal…to me. Now began my dazzling career as a real-life John Wayne.

The next six months or so offer nothing to make them stand out. There were constant small unit and company size patrols, mostly among the sameness of the hundreds of rice paddies of the Phu Nons. There were booby traps, the occasional sniper, and the less frequent fire fight. Men often died with no enemy in sight, no one to hold accountable, and no, as psychiatrist would say, closure. The frustration of seeing men die violently with no one to vent one's anger on is beyond explanation. You either understand it or you don't. Although I disapprove completely of the well-publicized massacre at My Lai 4, I certainly understand the frustration that can allow such a thing to happen in the absence of strong leadership. Once as we entered a village following the explosion of a command detonated mine in which one Marine had been blown into millions of small pieces, a young private came to me dragging an old "papa san". Apparently, I was the closest officer he could find and being a well-trained Marine, he asked permission to kill the old man. When I refused his request, he released his hold on the smiling, bowing old Vietnamese and went on about his duties.

One event which stands out vividly in my mind occurred as a result of an order to destroy rice crops in the fields to deny their use to the Vietcong. As a patrol I was with moved through the fields slicing down the ready to harvest rice with their machetes, a small girl ran awkwardly to me balancing a baby on her left hip. Looking first at the Marines in the rice paddy, she turned to me and said in a sad, heart-sick voice, "if you whack-whack, baby no chop-chop." To this day, even though I know much rice was left standing, the thought of that small girl and baby dying of starvation haunts me.

Another situation which left me with an overpowering feeling of waste concerned a young 2nd Lt. who joined my battalion several months after my arrival. At first meeting I was struck by how young and boyish he appeared. He was fair skinned and slightly chubby cheeked, and his enthusiasm gave evidence of his complete lack of understanding about combat.

This cherubic looking young man was supposed to take charge of a reinforced platoon stationed on a hill some distance from the battalion HQ and, turning down helicopter transportation, he began his journey in a truck convoy. Although the convoy was proceeded by combat engineers searching for mines, no one can find everything all the time, and no one found the large box mine which blew up the truck in which the young Lieutenant was riding. Thirteen days after leaving the States and his wife and small baby, the smiling, innocent Lieutenant was dead. His years of college, his intensive training by the Corps, his journey across the Pacific, all had come to nothing. The young Lieutenant never reached his first combat command.

Oddly enough, for all my desire to get into the air, one of my most vivid personal memories does involve an aircraft, a CH-46 Sea Knight helicopter.

My last few months in the bush were spent as the LO (Liaison Officer) for 3rd battalion, 5th Marines. One of my duties was to scout out locations for planned artillery fires in areas which the battalion would soon occupy. This was done by what we called a vertical recon. A VR was nothing more than flying in a helicopter at relatively low level and looking the ground over. On one of these flights we apparently disturbed some Vietcong during their lunch break and they opened up on the slow moving chopper with automatic weapons. As VC bullets came through the thin skin of the aircraft it occurred to me that there was no place to hide. On the ground I could always hit the deck and become as thin as possible. Here I could only stand and hope the next round would not make a future VR on my part unlikely.

Although the war would go on for several years after my tour ended, even in 1969 and 1970, there was a definite feeling that the country had given up on the war. No one liked the prospect of dying in a war that politicians, the omniscient press, some pampered college students, and the now predictable array of Hollywood "experts" had already surrendered to the enemy.

The strangeness of being in combat in a distant, Asian land and then returning home can be partly understood if one appreciates why vets referred to the United States as "the world." Some might think it was typical American egotism, but that totally misses the point. Vietnam was so far removed from what most of us had ever experienced that it was like another planet and leaving that planet to return home was going back to the world we knew. It was going back to a world where we fitted in, a world that was safe. It was going back to food and dress and customs we understood. It was going back to people we loved and who loved us. At least that's what we thought.

I flew home on Seaboard World Airways. Most of us were amazed at the age and size of some of the "stews" as we still called them. Word was that Seaboard had been a passenger line gone completely cargo that had returned to carrying passengers to cash in on the lucrative government contracts offered for flying returning vets home. The "stews", according to the scuttlebutt, were retreads from the line's previous passenger days. No matter, most of us were still unaccustomed to "round-eyes" so these looked pretty good.

My plane landed at Travis, AFB, in California, and that very night I got my first lesson in how much I had changed. To welcome me home in style, and probably because we were close to being strangers, my wife had made reservations for us at a popular local restaurant with a national reputation. It was amazing, in slow-motion, as I watched, people with enormous mouths and gaudy clothes stuffed prodigious quantities of food into their red, swollen faces with shovels. So many emaciated peasants in Vietnam lived on a few bowls of rice per day, and these over-fed, indulgent gluttons were wasting more food than a Vietnamese farmer would see in a month. My wife told me latter that I spent the evening looking slowly around the room with total hatred in my eyes. I do remember a strong desire to have, and use, an M-16, and deep shame at being a part of the scene. The dark, dingy pajamas of the peasants contrasted sharply with the bright colors of the diners, and the sight of so many elderly people trying to look and act half their age almost made me physical ill. It was not a good beginning, but it would get worse before it began to get better. To this day I am sickened by the waste and self-indulgence of many Americans.

Since I had leave before reporting for duty at Camp Pendleton, my wife and I headed east to visit my parents and hers. In New Jersey my in-laws put on a welcome home party for me. This was strange because I knew no one there except my wife and her parents, and I barely knew them.

We had wed in Oklahoma and her parents had not been able to attend. As far as I recall, I had met her mother less than a half dozen times, and her stepfather even fewer times than that. No one said much to me since they didn't know me. One man finally decided that someone should talk to the guest of honor, so he approached me awkwardly and asked how I liked being out of the Army. After I informed him that I was a Marine and still in the Corps, he mumbled something and made a hasty retreat. If anyone else talked to me that evening, I don't recall.

Someone, either my wife or her parents, decided that surely a military man, and history buff, would enjoy visiting the Gettysburg battlefield, a major turning point of the American Civil War. The whole experience of being on the ground that had produced over 50,000 casualties in three days of fighting preyed heavily on my mind and I said little. By the time we left New Jersey, my wife's parents probably thought she had married an emotional basket case. It is possible she shared their opinion.

It was during this time that a terrible thought began to well up in my mind; the realization that my entire value system and life plan had been radically altered. Fortunately, I still had a year left in the Corps, a year of cushion, a year of grace to gradually reenter my culture and attempt to rebuild, or replace, everything I had once believed in. Over the years I have come to appreciate how fortunate I truly was. In 1970 I was 25 years old, had a college degree and a year to try to sort things out. How difficult it must have been for a 19- or 20-year-old who had known nothing since high school but military training and war, and who found himself released from active service within days after leaving the rice paddies and jungles. American veterans of World War II were seen as warriors engaged in a noble cause and perhaps this eased their pain. Young men returning from Vietnam were not regarded as noble by many of their countrymen and were viewed as fair game for ridicule by some segments of the society. At best they were viewed neutrally, at worst as murderers and co-conspirators in a national disgrace. Men who have been in combat are never the same and the need to deal with the trauma of killing and death is real and pressing. Many Vietnam vets were returned to this country, thrown immediately back into civilian society, and never afforded that opportunity. To this day some are still paying the price. Others, like myself, were given a kind of military halfway house, a period of the familiar military customs and associations while we gingerly made our way back into the routines of civilian life.

Routine is probably the best way to describe civilian life after combat. When the implements of everyday life have consisted of rifle, helmet or bush hat, flak jacket, rucksack, etc., a lunch pail or briefcase seems dull by comparison. This isn't an attempt to glorify war, but a person is never more alive than when death is potentially seconds away. In Vietnam, in the bush, the possibility of death was a constant companion. There were so many ways a man could die: gunshot, booby trap, accident. Once, during the monsoon season, I stepped into what appeared to be just another shallow pool of water. As it turned out it was a water filled bomb crater and I remember the horror of trying to claw up the muddy side with pack, rifle, helmet, four canteens, boots, extra magazines of ammo and a flak jacket.

Not only was civilian life routine, it was frustrating. In combat problems are dealt with quickly and permanently. If an enemy soldier shoots at you and fails to kill you, you kill him. Problem solved. In civilian life such "problem solving" is regarded with some disfavor. In combat if you spot an enemy before he spots you, you shoot him...front or back, it makes no difference. In civilian life such action might be described by an unpleasant legal term...murder. For those young men who returned directly from combat to city streets it was difficult to make the adjustment, and it was asinine to assume they could. Even though my last several months in Vietnam were in a non-combat role, and even though I had almost a year stateside before being released into civilian life, I found the transition difficult; I can only imagine how hard it must have been for those who were literally given only days or weeks to successfully bridge the gap.

In addition to being routine and frustrating, civilian life proved to be inundated with trivial concerns. It is amazing how focused the mind becomes in a combat environment. There are few concerns about car payments, grocery shopping, light bills, gas bills, or any of the other worries that make up our lives in the hustle we refer to as civilization. In combat there is one overriding concern, staying alive. If you are still alive at the end of the day, then you had a good day; if you are still alive when morning comes, then you had a good night. It's simple and easily proven, you're either alive or you're not. If you're dead, you might wish you could argue that it isn't fair, that you only had three days left on your tour, that you weren't originally scheduled to be on the patrol on which you were killed, that your wife just had a baby, or whatever, but it doesn't matter. If you're dead, you're dead and no amount of arguing, if you could argue, will change it. Back in "the world" people argue over an assortment of things which seem so unimportant when compared to a situation of life or death. Yet readjustment to "normal" life means trying to learn again to associate importance with these unimportant bits of trivia. This ability to worry about such things is never completely regained and this, along with several other things, puts veterans out of step with others in society. In my own case this condition has persisted for 50 years.

For several years I was employed as a high school history teacher and my students were always amazed at the number of jobs I had held. The list, all since Vietnam, included such things as Marine, police officer, security guard, traveling salesman, industrial manager, schoolteacher, factory worker, janitor, and perhaps others I have forgotten. For over a decade after my return from Vietnam I did not realize that this unsettled nature and inability to stay with one job very long was a common trait among Vietnam vets. Perhaps some psychologist could attach a scientific name to it and offer a detailed explanation, I cannot. I only know that every few years I would have an overpowering need to be somewhere else, doing something else.

As mentioned, I still had a year in the Corps after my tour in Vietnam and this was spent at Camp Pendleton, about 100 miles south of Los Angles. Here I was assigned as the S-4 (Logistics Officer), for the 5th MAB (Marine Amphibious Brigade). This unit would serve as the base unit for the 1st Marine Division and would merge with that unit once the 1st MarDiv colors were returned to the United States. This interim period was to be of tremendous value in my readjustment. Since my wife and I lived off base, I was afforded the opportunity of a semi-civilian existence while still attached to the military for comfort and familiarity.

There is little about that time to distinguish it. I do recall talking to a younger Dan Rather who was present when the 1st MarDiv colors were returned stateside, and President Nixon came to honor the colors and the Corps. In addition, I did give thought to remaining in the Corps. A Major, Lt. Colonel, and Colonel offered to write letters of commendation to Headquarters Marine Corps on my behalf, but we were informed, due to the downsizing of the Corps, that it would do no good. Actually I didn't want to do another tour in Nam, a very real possibility, so the disappointment wasn't great.

After our discharge in 1971, my wife and I hitched a U-Haul trailer to our Mustang and headed for Colorado. The mountains and cool, dry air seemed a perfect backdrop for the rest of our lives. Surely there could be no better place to live than John Denver's Rocky Mountain High. Even in paradise one has to live however and finding a job did not prove easy. A degree in Speech and Drama and training as an infantry/artillery officer is not the best preparation for the civilian job market, especially when so many others had been drawn by the magic of the mountains.

Wherever I went the message was either overly qualified or not qualified at all. Eventually a job did surface working for a company that manufactured mobile homes. The hours were horrible however, and one day I learned that the Ft. Collins Police Department was hiring. It was certainly more professional than driving hundreds of screws day after day, and it did offer the comfort of a semi-military role, which I missed, so I applied.

The process involved interviews, a physical exam and background investigation. Before I found out I had gotten the job, an offer came through for a better paying job with Kodak. Although I tried to find out about the police position, no one could tell me, so I took the Kodak job. Three weeks later I was offered the job on the city police force. When I gave my notice at Kodak, the personnel officer made a point of telling me never to reapply.

One humorous incident did happen during those three weeks. I worked in the film packaging department which had only red lights and reflectors to work by and mark obstructions and doorways. The door I went through to get to the final packaging area was marked by a reflector on each side. One night, while I was on break, some maintenance worker had placed a reflector on a section of blocks which protruded out from the main wall. As I walked back in after being out in the light, I saw the first two sets of reflectors. Believing these to mark my doorway, I walked at full speed into a solid block wall. I heard my nose crack then, as I hit the floor, saw a beautiful display of stars. The plant nurse assured me I had suffered no injuries. Except for a broken nose and a possible concussion, I'm sure she was right.

After acceptance by the police department, the first order of business was the Colorado Law Enforcement Training Academy (CLETA). Here we learned the basics of law enforcement, then it was back to our individual departments for more local training and the experience of riding double with a fully qualified officer.

Police work, somewhat like combat, is hours and hours of tedium with those occasional incidents which make a person's heart pound out of their shirt. It also is an excellent way to study human nature, one's own as well as that of others.

There are few experiences to compare with entering the open back door of a business at 3:00 in the morning after the silent alarm has been activated on the dispatcher's console. It is also an interesting comment on human character when someone who is well known in the community reminds you of their supposed importance when you have stopped them for a traffic offence. Once, when I wrote a traffic ticket for the Athletic Director of Colorado State University, he informed me rather curtly that his buddy, the Police Chief, would void it.

On one occasion I was dispatched to a sorority house at Colorado State University to tell a coed that her mother had died. Apparently, the family had not been able to contact her and so had called the police to do the job. All the way there I rehearsed how to break the news to her gently and then be prepared for the flood of tears to follow. It was not something I looked forward to. When I entered the building and asked for the girl's room I was directed upstairs. When I knocked on the door, the girl opened it, took one look at me and said in a matter-of-fact tone, "mom's dead isn't she"? No tears, no breakdown, no words out of my mouth. I shook my head yes, she closed the door, I left.

During this time, I began to see that I was, as they say, wound pretty tightly.

The second weekend in May is College Days in Fort Collins. Students from all over the area come to drink, walk the streets, drink, crowd the bars, drink and, of course, drink. Although we generally patrolled in cars, on this occasion, some of us were on foot.

My partner and I were making bar checks of all the college bars when we came to one with a long line of people trying to get in. One young man in this line had long hair, a scraggly beard, and was wearing the blouse to the enlisted Marine dress blue uniform. I came unglued. Remembering so many young Marines who had worn that uniform with pride and then died in Vietnam, while this guy made a mockery of it, made me killing mad. My partner got hold of me and ushered me away before I did something that would have caused major problems, but the anger stayed with me for a long time.

Because of the silence imposed on Vietnam veterans by the society, most suffered for years believing they were the only ones who had to deal daily with the anger and frustration caused by a feeling of betrayal and rejection. This could, and frequently did, result in shame and loneliness difficult to describe. The first "peak" in this cycle, for me, occurred late one night in 1972. I came home from working the second shift with an intense feeling of worthlessness and emptiness. My beautiful wife lay asleep in the bedroom and suddenly I could think of no reason to remain alive. I sat down on the floor with my back braced against the wall. Taking my .38 from its holster, I cocked the hammer and placed the barrel in my mouth. I am alive today because of my belief in God and the values my parents had taught me. Had I not believed in the existence of an eternal being, and the strong desire not to hurt my Mom and Dad, I would be dead.

At this point a very strange thing occurred. As I began to remove the revolver from my mouth, I was shaking so badly that the possibility of accidentally killing myself became very real. I also became aware of the bitter, cold taste of the metal. Once I had safely removed the barrel, my thought turned to getting the hammer back down without accidentally discharging the weapon and having to explain what I was doing with it cocked in the first place. Once I had safely un-cocked the revolver, I sat shaking for some time, breathing rapidly and unable to think clearly. At least now I knew my faith would not allow me the cowards way out. No matter how deep the depression or anger became, I would have to deal with it the best I could.

It was also during this time that I began to hate people. Not specific people, but Americans in general. I hated them for their use and rejection of those of us who had served, for their gluttony and waste, for their shallowness and spoiled behavior, for their lack of concern for anything or anyone other than their next material acquisition, for their all-consuming preoccupation with the trivial and unimportant.

In 1973, at age 28, my first marriage fell apart. Divorce is something I did not, and do not, believe in, but I returned from a trip to see an ailing father to find that my wife of four years had filed for dissolution of marriage. Friends had picked me up in Denver and, when I asked why I had not been able to contact my wife, they gave me the news. In 1973 I learned that it was no longer necessary to give a reason why a divorce was wanted and that if one spouse wanted the marriage to end, the other could do nothing about it. For several months I remained in Colorado, but then returned to my family in Missouri.

In 1975, after completing course work necessary for teacher certification, I landed my first job as a history teacher in a small district south of Kansas City, Missouri. By this time, I had remarried and things should have been going well, but there was always a deep empty feeling like something valuable had been lost and nothing had taken its place. My sense of patriotism and desire to serve had been complete. When they were destroyed, I found a huge gap in my emotional makeup which I could not ignore.

My teaching job lasted two years and then a sense of restlessness came over me. The next five years saw me in a series of jobs.

If there are pivotal years in a person's life, 1983 was one of those years for me. That year I rejoined the military by way of the National Guard, started a new job, and found my second marriage ended, though divorce did not come for another three years.

Early in the year, for want of money, I had enlisted in a Guard unit and gone to training in Texas. Since I had enlisted in a station hospital unit, my training would be for 13 weeks at Fort Sam Houston as a combat medic. Most of the training emphasized the combat portion of the job description, rather than the medic portion, and it might be summed up by saying we were taught to take the wrapper off the band-aid before putting it on the wound.

Shortly after my return from Fort Sam, my unit was ordered to Fort Simmons Army Hospital in Colorado for two weeks of summer training. It was here that I came close to a complete breakdown.

There was nothing about the time at Fort Simmons that should have precipitated an emotional trauma, but perhaps it was the long period of time in uniform after so many years away from it. At any rate, I could feel myself slipping emotionally and I made an appointment with an Army psychologist. Here, for the first time, I discovered that others suffered the same problems that had plagued me for years. The psychologist offered me a piece of paper that listed all the symptoms I had. It literally amazed me that she knew exactly what I had been feeling. Then she explained that the list had been compiled as a result of similar sessions with other Vietnam combat veterans. In other words, what I had been experiencing was common to Vietnam vets, and I was not the oddity I thought myself to be.

Since my unit had only a few days left before returning to its home base, the psychologist told me about a service for Vietnam vets, run by Vietnam vets, and found in various malls in cities around the country. It happened that there was one in Kansas City and she gave me the number to call to get the address. When I asked for a copy of the list I had looked at, she asked if I had driven my own vehicle to summer training or had come in a convoy. When I answered that I had driven, she refused. She told me bluntly that she feared I would pull off the side of the road, begin to read the information, become depressed and hurt myself. She had no way of knowing that I had already settled that question in my mind and that suicide was not an option for me.

Shortly after returning to the Kansas City area, I contacted the Vietnam Vets Storefront Center and made an appointment. Soon I was to find out, again, the difficulties Vietnam vets faced in even attempting to deal with their emotions in a positive way.

On the day of my appointment, I walked into the office in a small strip mall in Kansas City. At the desk I told a young man who I was and gave him the name of the man I was to see. It happened that the man with whom I had an appointment was walking out as I was walking in. He gave me an agitated look and told me to accompany him to his office. There he motioned to a chair and, as he loosened his tie, called someone on the phone and told them he would not be able to join them for lunch because something had come up. This seemed strange to me since I had arrived at the time set by the office for my appointment.

Next, I noticed his youth and commented on how young he must have been during his Vietnam service. He informed me that not only was he not a veteran of Vietnam, but that his only experience with the military had been a short enlistment in the National Guard. There was no way he could understand anything I was feeling, so I left.

Once again, I felt betrayed. The program I had been told was run by Vietnam vets for Vietnam vets, was nothing more than the standard bureaucratic rip-off. Some young men who knew nothing of the experiences of combat veterans were being paid to sit, listen, and act as if they really cared and understood. What their advice could have been is completely beyond me. It's a little like asking a 10-year-old girl to counsel a 30-year-old woman whose only child has just been stillborn.

Now my confusion increased. I knew others were experiencing the same ripping emotions as myself but did not know what to do about it since my avenue of help had turned out to be a dead end.

It was also during this time that I began to feel guilty. The guilt came partly from the fact that I had not been physically wounded, and partly because my combat experience, though very real, had been slight in comparison with many others. How did I have the right to feel as I did? Surely, since I had no physical wounds and limited combat, I should be able to go on with life without any feelings at all about Vietnam. There must be some singular failing in myself, some deficiency of character. But how did I deal with the strong sense of being out of step with the world around me?

Through some process I no longer remember, I ended up at the Veterans Hospital in Kansas City, Missouri. The first doctor I encountered in the outpatient psychiatric wing of the hospital was a young man who began explaining his group therapy program to me. Perhaps he was trying to weed out imposters, so he explained how readily the members of the group could spot a phony. He told about one man who had joined the group but had not known the standard term used by infantrymen in Vietnam for a backpack. Although I had lived out of one for months, until he said "rucksack", I couldn't have thought of the word if my life had depended on it. It occurred to me then that this group was partly playing word games, and I wondered how many of them were impostors. He also told me, like so many others, about a relative who had served in Vietnam but, alas, he had not had the opportunity.

It didn't take me long to decide that sitting around, spilling my guts to a bunch of strangers I didn't trust, was not for me. Eventually I wound up in the office of one of the psychiatrists who became my confidant for the next several years.

At this point I should explain that even admitting there was a problem, much less seeking help, was a difficult step for me. I had been raised to believe that people should take care of their own problems and that psychiatry was, for the most part, the resort of weak, self-indulgent people. But I had come to the point in my life where it was necessary to have help simply to understand the myriad of unfamiliar emotions that seemed to have taken control of me.

For several years I made regular visits to the VA hospital to talk and get my prescription for antidepressants refilled. During all this time I was never able to really open up the way I wanted to and talk about the deep-seated loss

I felt or the growing sense of distrust I felt for all authority figures. The truth is, I didn't even trust the doctor who was supposed to help me deal with my lack of trust.

As the years went by, just functioning from day to day seemed to require all the energy I possessed. At the end of the workday I felt so drained that frequently I had to sit for a long period of time before I could even drive home or complete other necessary tasks. I also felt an overpowering need to talk to another Vietnam veteran about my feelings, and an almost palpable antagonism when talking to other men of my age who had not served in the war.

Since over three million military personnel served in Southeast Asia during the war, it might seem that finding one to talk to would be easy. However, one must understand that, even in wartime, only about ten to fifteen percent of those in uniform ever serve in combat; the remainder serve in support roles. I have no desire to belittle the contributions of non-combat personnel, but I have personally been told by some that the year they spent in Vietnam was a very pleasant experience for them. I recall one such vet telling me how desperately he tried to extend his tour but was not allowed to. In actuality only about 500,000 vets served in combat, and finding one is not all that easy. This is especially true given the attitude of the American public for many years and the need to keep one's service in Vietnam quiet.

As for my antagonism toward those of my age who did not serve, it is still strong even though I fight to suppress it. When I see these men, I wonder what they did to avoid service. Did they run off to Canada, manipulate the draft system, hurriedly get married or start a family? What method did they employ to preserve themselves from service, avoiding legal action, while others of us died or experienced things that would mar us for life? President Carter's blanket pardon of those who ran off to Canada did nothing to help this feeling. Later, the discovery that President Clinton had manipulated the draft system to preserve his precious life did nothing to soften the blow.

Were those of us who served stupid to believe the propaganda about patriotism? Did we just show our gullibility when we believed, as Americans, that service to our country was a responsibility we all had?

With the fighting in recent years and months, I see again the seeds of depression and rejection for another generation. Second guessing by some in the press, failure to support troops while claiming to do so on the part of some politicians, and the assumption by some in the entertainment industry that they understand something about which they know little or nothing, again sets the stage for undermining those who are willing to put everything on the line for their country.

Americans seem unable to accept the realities of a post atomic bomb world where the likelihood of a conflict such as World War II is remote. But since there will always be psychopaths, such as Hitler, who manage to acquire power, there will always be the necessity of dealing with them militarily. These conflicts will never produce the nice, clean, tidy endings so favored by Americans. Such conflicts will be hazy, muddled, confused. Fighting an enemy who recognizes few, if any, rules, will cause the infantryman to rely more and more on the only two rules which really matter to the man at the front with a rifle in his hands: stay alive, keep your buddies alive. All the other rules will be left to the Monday morning quarterbacks who know exactly what should have been done by a man whose life hung in the balance. If he reacted a split second too late, or pondered the rules a little too long, he would die or be the cause of a buddy going home in a body bag. William Fairbairn, a famous World War II hand-to-hand combat instructor, once said that there was no such thing as fair play, and that the only rule was kill or be killed.

Contrary to what Americans like to believe, infantrymen have always been reduced to the level of semi-animal. Vietnam was not the first war fought in living, or dying, color. Nor was it the first U.S. conflict in which "atrocities" were committed. Audie Murphy, America's most decorated soldier of World War II, openly stated in his autobiography, *To Hell and Back*, that his first two "kills" were Italian soldiers he shot in the back. Of course, there were no reporters present to record this horrible deed in living color for broadcast on the nightly news that very evening. There were no high profile "anchors" to report it with solemn face and furrowed brow. There were no morning talk show hosts to spend fifteen minutes dissecting the action of a millisecond, committed by a man whose stress level had been on the ragged edge for days or weeks. None of these "experts" were there to demand an immediate investigation and so Murphy went on to a glorious combat career topped by winning the Congressional Medal of Honor. A career that included the killing of almost 200 Italian and German soldiers.

In Vietnam and subsequent conflicts, there have been terrible stories about "friendly fire" incidents. Again, it is almost as if the press is unaware that such events have been a part of every war ever fought. In the Civil War, before uniforms were standardized, Union troops fired on Union troops, and Confederates fired on Confederates. In World War II, after the weather cleared in the last days of the Battle of the Bulge, American bombers, due to a wind shift, dropped bombs on American troops killing over 500 of their own. But again, no press reported these admittedly tragic events as if they had never occurred before. Perhaps those reporters realized that not all accidents are minor and painless and, as callous as it may sound, such things will always be a part of war.

As the reader can tell, I am tired of being a Vietnam veteran. Tired of the service I offered with honor and integrity being held up as the equivalent of the town drunk, an example of what not to do and how not to do it. Tired of hearing some all-knowing newsman or woman voice the fear that some conflict may become "another Vietnam". Tired of entertainment personalities abusing their access to the American public to promote their own, sometimes, twisted social agenda as if they really believe that freedom can come at little or no cost and without a single unpleasant occurrence to mar the beauty of the victory. It would be wonderful if the human family could settle differences in ways that left no losers or hurt feelings. Unfortunately, that has never happened in all recorded history and never will, no matter what the Hollywood "children" like to pretend or no matter how much the all-knowing talk show hosts and news personalities like to pontificate.

Recently I celebrated my 75th birthday. The last 50 of those years have been lived under a shadow. Sometimes I tell myself how ridiculous that is. It doesn't help. Sometimes I tell myself to just forget it. That doesn't help either.

Vietnam is a daily experience. I walk through a beautiful park area, notice a hill, and begin deciding where to place machine guns to achieve an interlocking field of fire. I see a war movie and notice the soldiers are walking so close together that one grenade could take out several. I remember the little boy who offered to sell me his mother after assuring me she was a virgin. I remember the little girl eating from a garbage pile while holding off two equally hungry little boys with a pocketknife. I remember a young Marine moaning with a head wound while we waited for a chopper on a pitch-black night. I remember holding a Marine in my arms while he died after his jeep hit a road mine. I remember a chopper crewman twirling the remains of one of our Marines like a top before flipping the almost empty body bag onto the cargo floor of his chopper. I remember jumping behind a huge bolder as shrapnel came whistling by. I remember solid red ropes streaking from the sky as an AC130 fired Gatling guns. I remember the shock when I learned that a young Marine I knew well had been blown in half by a reversed claymore. I remember operations in the Arizona, a free fire zone where anything that moved was fair game. I remember a CH-46 helicopter landing in our company area to deliver a cake. It was 10 November 1969, the 194th birthday of the Corps. I remember the 24/7 stress and fatigue.

Today when I look at my country, I am shocked and saddened. Pampered over paid athletes refuse to respect the flag that many have fought for and many died for. Politicians spout dogma that would destroy the very uniqueness of the country that has been the destination for multiple millions of people from all over the world. Socialism and communism are spoken of as genuine alternatives to democracy. Freedom of speech exists only for those with the "correct" views. The country is divided and full of hate. We are on the verge of destroying the greatest experiment in human history.

Some time back I asked my sister if she had noticed any difference in me since I returned from Vietnam. She replied, "The man who returned from Vietnam was not my brother."

SHADOWS IN POETRY AND PROSE

It hangs suspended,
Upside down,
Against the wall.
This almost violent token of the past.
A toy gun cut from an old man's love and time and wood.

Some parts too small, some too big. Yet the overall effect is that of "gun."

So armed I have led cavalry across the yard and routed Indians hiding in ambush by the shed.

So armed I have learned the "romance" of war, and the "glory" of dying young.

The incongruity is almost too much to bear;
Loving and caring;
Killing and dying.

At first it bore a certain charm,
the buliet strikes, the flying mud
as he lay flatter still and thought…
so this is war?

The fear and heat gnawed at his soul,
out there on that last patrol,
and then the jungle came alive…
so this is war!

He fired his rounds, he yelled distain,
as if it all were just a game,
and then the bullet found its mark…
so this is war?!

At first there was no pain at all,
then came the searing flame within
igniting organs, bone and skin…
So this is war!

He journeyed home to be with kin,
they took one last look, and then
buried him among his friends…
That is war!!

The metal taste was cold and sharp,
and sent shivers through my soul
　　How could I take the coward's way,
but how could I grow old?

　　How could I face so many days
knowing what I had done?
　　How could I walk with head held high
when I only dished to run?

　　And now so many years have passed,
long days followed on,
　　And I have smiled and laughed and loved,
as though t'were nothing wrong.

　　The faces still are bright and clear,
though half a century gone,
　　Their bodies crumpled in the mud,
their lives so early done.

　　Each day I rise and wonder why
I live and they should die.
　　Am I really the lucky one
or should I bow and cry?

W e took the walk late one evening toward the end of my leave. Our route and pace took us slowly down the block in the direction of town, four left turns, then back home. When it ended, we had circled the block and the basic arrangements for my funeral and burial had been made. Although statistics were on my side, a strange feeling persisted that I would not return alive and it didn't seem wise to leave such an issue unresolved. It's amazing how the mind and body can disassociate from one another. As I described to my father what to do with my body, it seemed only that I was taking care of sad but necessary business for a friend. Specifics about the casket and burial plot were just part of that service.

My father and I had left the house that night because I did not want to upset my mother. Oddly, the thought of upsetting my father never occurred to me. Combat was a man thing and so men should discuss its possible consequences. Even though my father and I had never been particularly close, this was something I felt we shared. At 23 years of age, I was quite convinced of the correctness of this approach.

The cemetery in Lawson occupied a few acres on the southeast corner of town. As a young boy my friends and I had occasionally played games of dare in the early evening hours. Courage could be shown by lying face down on a grave. If the grave was fresh, the sense of courage was heightened. I wondered how many young boys would lie face down on my grave, breathing rapid and shallow, hearts pounding. I wondered if it would be long before they would have the chance to do it.

The remainder of my leave passed with that false sense of happiness experienced by all families in those circumstances. The smiles seemed carefully arranged, the laughter forced. No one was supposed to acknowledge that we might never have the chance to smile or laugh together again.

A year later I would return to that same small town. Through firefights, exhausting days, and tense nights, I had not received a single wound. Around me men had died, and I had killed some, but there would be no burial at an early age. There would be the guilt of knowing others rested in those premature graves while I had the opportunity to grow old, and the question that would never go away, "why?".

Shadows flow through the damaged mind
    shadows of every type and kind.
Shadows of what happened then and
    shadows of what might have been.

Perhaps that one didn't have to die,
    he seemed so to say by his gentle cry.
His eyes said he wanted to live so much,
    and feel the softness of a woman's touch.

Children might have graced his life
    with the companionship of a loving wife.
His life would have filled with Joy and tears,
    and the memories as he gathered years.

Now his body lies on the muddy ground.
    brought to naught by one distant sound.
One rifle crack from way beyond.
    and all that might have been is gone.

Sometimes it's difficult to say
    what the soul needs so to say
About the loss that won't return
    once it has gone away,
About the burning sense of pain
    that grows from deep within
Some part of the spirit's dead
    and will not live again
War does such damage to the mind
    and kills some human part
And all that's left is a damaged soul
    and the remains of a damaged heart
Someday, perhaps, the pain will cease
    and the heart will live again
Someday, perhaps, the soul will heal
    but what of life till then?

A bedroom celling on a pitch-black night is an excellent place to study one's past. No exaggerations, no excuses: the mind will allow no such interference when there is no one to impress or refute. Instead there are the numerous failures and downfalls interspersed with just the right amount of success to avoid complete debilitating depression.

There was "the dream". A life plan so magnificent it filled the dreamers every thought and breath for eight full years yet shattered to an ending leaving the dreamer adrift in a sea of uncertainty and misdirection.

There was the unpopular war fought by the dreamer. All the John Wayne experiences without the bright lights or applause. Nothing but the smell of death and betrayal and a country the dreamer no longer trusted.

Then of course the sense of being constantly out of step. Unable to identify with men with the same number of years but not the same mind and body altering experiences. A feeling of interacting with children who insist they understand when all their language says they haven't a clue.

Perhaps the dreamer has led two lives: LBW and LAW. Life Before War is full of dreams with nothing to dim the possibility of their glorious realization. Life After War is constantly chasing the dreams as they skip among the clouds of regret and recrimination. LAW means accepting that something was lost which will never be retrieved. And most painfully, the dream itself eventually becomes lost in other dreams that make it appear only in brief, indefinable glimpse, just enough to remind the dreamer that there was a dream.

Somewhere in the maze there lies a key.
Behind a troubled thought
    discolored image
    contorted dream, it hides.
An answer:
    a solution
    a map of all of life and all its loss or gain.
Perhaps it has already come to view and been tossed
    aside as worthless.
Perhaps the rest of life is…looking for the key already
found?

No time to mourn the dead Marine
    killed by an enemy still unseen.
No time for council to express one's grief,
    only the feeling of guilty relief
    that the bullet found another mark.

No time to wonder what might have been
    had he lived his life to a normal end.
Generations that won't be born
    'cause he died in the mud
    on this filthy morn.

Perhaps back home there's a waiting wife
    or a mother aged beyond her years,
And soon the word will seek them out
    and their world will end in a flood of tears,
    their hopes and dreams are dead.

But now there's no thought of what's to come
    or his folks back home who await their son
Or a wife who longs for him to arrive
    only the thought
    I'm still alive!

The "crack" was unmistakable. Sharp, like a spear point. Instinctively, I drop to the prone position, "16" lying across my arms, trying to melt into the ground. I begin to crawl toward the sound, checking the perimeter for any movement that would indicate an attempt to breech our lines. Would there be more fire, or was this just another way the VC would use to keep us on edge, make us lose sleep?

But something is wrong. Everything is hazy, not quite in focus. Where is the perimeter? Where are the other Marines, the Gunny, the CO? Why is no one returning fire? Why no muzzle flashes, fire shooting across the ground? Why the complete silence?

Something's wrong with the ground. There's no dampness. There's no breeze bringing in that horrible smell of rot and filth. No clothes clinging to me from days and days of sweat and stress.

Then, through my pounding heart and watery eyes reality crashes in like the chainsaw killer in some horror film. I stand up but still crouching. Slowly and quietly, I slink back to the bed and crawl in beside my still sleeping wife. Maybe she didn't hear, maybe she doesn't know. She probably already thinks I'm crazy enough without this.

My breathing slows down, my body relaxes a little. If she just doesn't wake up for a while, I won't have to explain why I'm cold and clammy. The truth comes over me like a brisk wind on a cold, overcast winter day and I shake. This isn't 'Nam, this is a motel room in New Mexico.

He was pink cheeked, fair skinned, and had an air of enthusiasm about him that spoke volumes. His eager voice and grin said he understood nothing of the filth, confusion, and finality of Vietnam combat Only a few days before he had left the States and his wife and new baby and now he was here in "the Nam" to put his nine months of training to the test He was a 2nd Lieutenant of Marines.

The battalion was temporarily assigned the duty of guarding Liberty Road which ran from the mountains, over a river and on into Da Nang. There were three hills, each smaller than the one before, which were used to guard the road. A reinforced platoon occupied the smallest hill, a reinforced company the middle hill, and the remainder of the battalion guarded the largest of the three. After a few days to become familiar with the Area of Operations, the new infantry lieutenant would be given command of the Marines on the smallest hill.

For three days the Lieutenant studied situation maps, rules of engagement, etc., then came time for him to make the trek to his first command. As LO for the battalion, I frequently made what we called "vertical recons" of the area held by the enemy. This involved flying at low altitude and attempting to observe signs of enemy activity so I could plan artillery and air strikes. On the day the lieutenant was to journey to the smallest of the hills, I had such a flight planned. Since the chopper could get him to the hill fast,

I offered him a ride. He opted instead to take a truck convoy in order to get a feel for the terrain from the infantry point of view. This made perfectly good sense and I bid him goodbye and good luck as my chopper lifted off.

Truck convoys were preceded by combat engineers who swept the road for mines and other booby traps. These men knew their job and did it well, but no one is perfect. Perhaps the box mine was pressure detonated, perhaps command detonated, it really makes no difference. The six-by the lieutenant was riding in detonated the explosive with one of the rear wheels. The lieutenant, who normally would have been riding in the cab, had chosen to ride in the bed for a better view of the terrain. Everyone in the bed was killed or seriously injured. The lieutenant was among the former. Exactly thirteen days from the day he had kissed his wife and baby goodbye, the smiling, exuberant, pink-cheeked lieutenant was dead. His years of college and nine months of extensive Marine training had never been used. He never reached his first command.

Today, half a century later, I can still see his smile and hear his voice, but I can't remember his name.

His son is approaching middle age. I wonder what he knows of the father he never knew?

                              deep
within   some
recess   of my   mind
              there
        lies   a   thought
a   word
a   feeling   that I
                              long to
        find   but   days
                                      have passed and
                                      weeks
and   months and   years
and   the   lost
        lies   hidden
some   where
within   my   tears

I could never tell their ages.

For some reason these small, olive-skinned, beautiful Vietnamese children always looked younger than they actually were; this little girl was no exception. One thing was certain, she couldn't possibly be the mother of the doll like, big-eyed baby balanced on her left hip.

We had been ordered to destroy much of the rice crop surrounding her little village and Marines were busy with their machetes.

Viet Cong operating in the area were stealing the rice crop from the villagers and using it to sustain themselves as they waged their hit and run war against the Americans. They were sometimes brutal in their treatment of the villagers but now the little girl must have thought there was no way they could win; either the VC stole it, or we destroyed it.

As the girl walked to me with her burden of love clinging to her wet, pajama like clothing, she knew nothing of the global significance of the military contest being waged around the village, she saw only the destruction of the food the baby needed in order to live.

"You whack-whack, baby no chop-chop".

Tens of thousands of innocent German women and children were killed by the carpet bombing of World War II, and tens of thousands more died in the fire and atomic bombing of Japan; but this was different. This little girl stood only a few feet away. This little girl was looking into my eyes.

How could I respond to her soft objection? How could I remind her that if we didn't destroy it, the Viet Cong would steal it? How could I tell her that well fed VC meant more dead Marines? She understood only the tiny baby she carried.

The machetes continued their work and the little girl followed me around without speaking. There was no accusation in her eyes, no anger. Even in her short life she had learned to accept the inevitable. War had been her daily companion since birth.

Marines were taking breaks from their work in the hot, sticky day, gulping warm water from their plastic canteens. A thick, sickening liquid that hit the stomach with all the delicacy of a brick. The little girl stood a few feet from me, looking. No quivering mouth, no tears, just the question posed by her eyes.

We finished our work and moved out of the village. There would be similar work in similar villages, interspersed with fire fights and booby traps. There would be wounded Marines and dead Marines. I might be one of them, I might not.

The girl looked, the baby clung to her, the eyes asked their question, I had no answer, we moved on.

Hours spent quiet
    in a darkened room
It could be morning
    or night or noon

The mind is lost
    in a cold, dark mist
In some other world
    or maybe this

Thoughts flow through
    on phantom wings
And fears roar by
    with bites and stings

The pains we had
    in that other life
Lay waste our souls
    like a cold, dull knife

Fear can work its way from the depth of your soul to your eyebrows, toes, and fingertips. Fear can kill you or it can keep you alive. Lying there in the mud I hoped it would serve me in the latter fashion.

We had taken fire from the village on several occasions and the decision had been made, by those who make such decisions, to encircle it in the dark and sweep through it at first light. Probably looked great on paper but moving 130 or so Marines through rice paddies and deploying them when they could barely see their hands six inches in front of their eyes was a little more challenging. I doubted that the villagers had much of a surprise in store. I only hoped we didn't.

Village. Strange label for a small collection of open-sided, thatch-roofed huts on a little patch of raised ground encircled by endless rice paddies. No stores, schools, churches. No tree lined streets. No cars, telephones, TV antennas. Nothing but mud floored huts, the scent of wet coals in last night's cook fires, and the gut level stench of human and animal excrement. I remembered all the times the "mamasans" had squatted by the side of the road and urinated or defecated as we walked by on patrol. Each time they would flash a big black-toothed grin and shout "Maline numba one"! I wondered how many were expressing their real sentiment by their activity, and how many were deadly proficient with an AK-47.

Soon it would be time to go "over the top" and each second I was developing a greater respect for the trench soldiers of World War I. Some villagers were beginning to stir. Cooking fires were being prodded into life and the scrawny birds that passed for chickens were squawking their objection to another day. Would the next few minutes find us in a blazing gun battle, automatic weapons pouring out their deafening roar, or would we just look like a bunch of silly, over-loaded, over-armed Americans?

The signal is given. I scramble up the mud slope, loose my footing and fall flat on my face. I guess a "Hero" label is out of the question.

It is totally quiet. No rifle fire, no machine guns, no grenades. Just perpetually bowing "mamasans" and "papasans". Suddenly I feel like an intruder who has broken down a kitchen door just as the family was sitting down to breakfast. Rather than anger I am greeted by smiles and apparent apologies for not having set a plate for me.

After searching the village, we trudge off, boots laden with mud and excrement, tired beyond belief.

Another fruitless operation. One of many.

The knot in the pit of my stomach begins to loosen.

When I see them today with their long hair, unkept beards, and a pot belly, wearing an old uniform that cannot bridge the gap, it makes me sad and ill. Marching in welcome home parades that are 50 years too late seems such an unfunny joke and makes me feel ashamed.

Half a century ago these same men marched in crisp precision wearing creased uniforms that fit smoothly over muscled stomachs. Today they are in formation only in the sense that they are in roughly the same place, headed in roughly the same direction.

Since I would never participate in such a demeaning charade, I wonder what makes these men willing to do so. Are they so hungry for some display of understanding and belated appreciation that they will settle for this march down main street while spectators make insulting, disrespectful comments about their totally non-military appearance?

Perhaps these men are the non-combat types who spent their tours inside heavily guarded compounds with their air-conditioned hooch's, refrigerators, closets full of starched jungle utilities and spit shined jungle boots, nice cots, and their loved one's pictures on the wall. One veteran I talked to told me he had been issued an M-16 on the day of his arrival in country and had not touched it again until he turned it in at the conclusion of his tour. Another told me how scared he had been when a VC rocket landed

61

within a half mile of his hooch. In the bush a half mile might as well have been another galaxy.

No matter who these men are or what their service might have been, I am deeply saddened at the sight. They deserved better and they deserved it at the proper time.

ABOUT THE AUTHOR

Doyle Harrison Wyatt was born on May 22, 1945, during the last days of WWII. He was the product of poor people from the hills of Arkansas who put a premium on service to GOD, hard work and patriotism. His service in Vietnam and the reaction of some Americans to that service left an impression on Mr. Wyatt that continues to this day.